The Inner Smile

Increasing Chi through
the Cultivation of Joy

Mantak Chia

Destiny Books
Rochester, Vermont

Destiny Books
One Park Street
Rochester, Vermont 05767
www.DestinyBooks.com

Destiny Books is a division of Inner Traditions International

Originally published in Thailand in 2005 by Universal Tao Publications under the title *Cosmic Inner Smile: Smile That Heals*

Library of Congress Cataloging-in-Publication Data
Chia, Mantak, 1944–
  [Cosmic inner smile]
  The inner smile : increasing chi through the cultivation of joy / Mantak Chia.
     p. cm.
  Originally published: Cosmic inner smile
  Includes index.
  ISBN: 978-1-59477-155-2
  1. Taoism. 2. Hygiene, Taoist. I. Title.
  BL1920.C2576 2008
  299.5'14—dc22
                                                              2008004647
Printed and bound in India by Replika Press Pvt. Ltd.

10   9

Text design by Priscilla Baker
Text layout by Virginia Scott Bowman
This book was typeset in Janson with Present and Futura as display typefaces

Contents

Putting the Inner Smile into Practice

The practices described in this book have been used successfully for thousands of years by Taoists trained by personal instruction. Readers should not undertake the practices without receiving personal transmission and training from a certified instructor of the Universal Tao, since certain of these practices, if done improperly, may cause injury or result in health problems. This book is intended to supplement individual training by the Universal Tao and to serve as a reference guide for these practices. Anyone who undertakes these practices on the basis of this book alone does so entirely at his or her own risk.

The meditations, practices, and techniques described herein are *not* intended to be used as an alternative or substitute for professional medical treatment and care. If any readers are suffering from illnesses based on mental or emotional disorders, they should consult an appropriate professional health care practitioner or therapist. Such problems should be corrected before you start training.

This book does not attempt to give any medical diagnosis, treatment, prescription, or remedial recommendation in relation to any human disease, ailment, suffering, or physical condition whatsoever.

Neither the Universal Tao nor its staff and instructors can be responsible for the consequences of any practice or misuse of the information contained in this book. If the reader undertakes any exercise without strictly following the instructions, notes, and warnings, the responsibility must lie solely with the reader.

What Is the Universal Tao?

The Universal Tao is a self-help system for curing and preventing illness and stress, and for enhancing all aspects of life. Its key concept is increasing vital energy, or chi, through easy techniques and physical exercises. This life-force energy is then circulated through the acupuncture meridians of the body and channeled into health, vitality, balanced emotions, and creative and spiritual expression.

A practical system accessible to everybody, the Universal Tao is a modern expression of Taoist practices that are centuries old. Many of these techniques were formerly known only to an elite group of Taoist masters and hand-picked students. I have formulated these powerful practices into a comprehensive system, which I began teaching to the public at large in my native Thailand in 1973. In 1978, I brought this system to the Western world. I then opened the Universal Tao Center in New York and began teaching the practices there. Today, we teach our system in various places throughout the United States and Europe. Though spiritual in its foundation, the Universal Tao is not a religion. It is compatible with all religions, as well as with agnosticism and atheism. There are no rituals to perform and no gurus to surrender to. The master and the teacher are highly respected, but they are not deified.

The entire system of the Universal Tao has three levels:

1. Level I concentrates on universal energy, strengthening and calming the body.
2. Level II concentrates on changing negative emotions into strong, positive energy.
3. Level III concentrates on creative and spiritual practices.

This book presents a detailed description and instructions for the Inner Smile meditation, an essential beginning practice for Level I of the system. All levels include both mental (meditative) practices and physical disciplines, such as Tai Chi, Pakua, and Iron Shirt Chi Kung. The foundation course called the Microcosmic Orbit is covered in my first book, *Awaken Healing Energy Through the Tao,* but is also summarized in this book as part of a daily practice. For a description of other courses and for the addresses and phone numbers of the Universal Tao centers, visit the Web site given at the end of this book.

TAOISM AND SOME BASIC CONCEPTS IN CHINESE HEALING

Taoism is the foundation of Chinese philosophy and medicine developed over 5,000 to 8,000 years of study and observation. It is also the mother of acupuncture and the inspiration for modern body-oriented therapies, such as acupressure, Rolfing, and the Feldenkrais method. The Tao has been described as "natural law" or "natural order," "the constantly changing cycle of the seasons," "an art," "a method," "a power," and "a path of direction."

In the Taoist view, harmony and balance are essential for health. Taoists see the body as a whole; therefore, stress or injury to one organ, gland, or system weakens the entire body. The body is also self-regulating and will naturally move toward balance if allowed to.

Illness is caused by a blockage of energy. Too much or too little energy in one part of the body results in disease to that part and stresses the entire body. The Universal Tao teaches us how to correct this imbalance by awakening the chi, or vital energy, and circulating it to the needed areas.

The Taoist system links each organ to one of the five elements in nature: metal, water, wood, fire, and earth. It also connects them to a season of the year, a color, and a quality in nature (wet, dry, warm, windy, etc.). This relationship often describes the characteristics of that organ. For example, the heart is linked to summer, fire, and red; a healthy heart is associated with excitement and warmth. The season of an organ is the one in which the organ is dominant or working the hardest.

Body, mind, and spirit are totally integrated in the Taoist view. Therefore, Chinese medicine finds that negative emotions, such as anger, fear, or cruelty, and excessive amounts of positive emotions, such as too much joy or excitement, can injure the organs and cause disease. Both the Inner Smile (covered in this book) and the Six Healing Sounds (covered in other Universal Tao books) help to balance the emotions as well as to improve health. For complete instructions on the Six Healing Sounds, see *Six Healing Sounds*.

ILLNESS STARTS AS A PROBLEM WITH THE ENERGY LEVEL

A problem may exist for many years before it physically manifests as a disease. The problem may appear as a blockage or as a decrease of the chi energy level, leading to a chi imbalance in particular parts or organs of the body. If we become aware of the chi imbalance when it first occurs, we have a long grace period in which to correct it.

Many people don't regard bad temper or negative emotions as sickness. In Taoism, we regard these as the beginning of the imbalance of the chi energy in the system, just as bad breath or body odor can be the beginning signs of weakness or illness of the liver, kidneys, or stomach.

Stubbornness can be caused by an imbalance of the heart energy. Malodorous sweat can be due to a dysfunction of the kidneys, which have lost the filtering function to eliminate excess water contained in the body fluids. Cowardice and fear can be due to an imbalance of the lung or kidney energy. Back pain can be caused by an imbalance of the kidneys and bladder. And we can trace many other unwanted behaviors and physical ailments to an imbalance of the chi energy in different parts of the body.

Nowadays, as we live our lives, our attachment to the material world grows and we become more and more drawn to material things as well as various drugs, entertainment, services, and unnatural foods. The more we feel that we need to have this and buy that, the more worry and mixed emotions we feel. We can get rid of all of these feelings by getting rid of our emotional attachment to these materials.

Conserving, increasing, and transforming the chi energy should be the first or primary preventive method we practice. When a person has a heart attack, he or she might use this method to prevent a second. When a bad kidney or bad back develops, using this method prevents it from getting worse. We start the primary preventive practices at the chi level. In the Taoist system, we map out all the organ energy meridians, which have a network extending from the organs throughout the body. When chi is blocked or decreased, the organs are the parts that will get less life force and will trap the bad chi (i.e., the chi we know as sick energy in the organs or the meridians). If we are not in touch with our inner selves, it is very hard to notice much change internally. When we know how to conserve, transform, and increase the chi, we have more chi to open the blockage, increase the body's defensive powers, and prevent illness. We can live the happy, healthy life we want to live and maintain our health as we age; we can live life not going from one illness to another, but instead having life-long vitality and a will (desire) to live.

The Taoist system is geared to help you live a healthy life, free from illness, with vitality to help other fellow human beings. Many of my students have given up coffee, alcohol, drugs, and certain kinds of "necessary" entertainment quite easily when they started to work on themselves to satisfy their organs and senses and thereby strengthen them.

I have one student who, at one time, employed many factory workers and, therefore, had power over many people. However, he was deeply in debt because he couldn't give up endlessly buying things. Finally, he came to me and talked about his problem. I explained to him that stress and emotional energy created blockages due to energy imbalances in his organs. If he could strengthen his organs and senses and increase the circulation in his body, he would see the world from a different angle. After he completed the Microcosmic Orbit meditation and practiced the Six Healing Sounds, Inner Smile, and Tao Rejuvenation, he came to me and said, "Master Chia, I'm going on a long vacation." I asked, "What happened?" He replied that he had sold his factory, paid all of his debts, and had a few thousand dollars left. "I want to rest, practice more of what you teach, and come back and start all over again." There was a tremendous change in his face.

WHAT IS CHI?

Perhaps the most basic and general principle of Taoist thought is the concept of chi. Its status in Chinese philosophy is developed in the popular works of Lao Tzu (604–511 BCE) and Chuang Tzu (399–295 BCE), but its origins go back much farther. The word *chi* has many translations, such as energy, air, breath, wind, vital breath, vital essence, and so forth. Although difficult to define, it can be thought of as the activating energy of the universe.

Chi condenses and disperses in alternating cycles of negative and positive (yin and yang) energy, materializing in different ways, forms, and shapes. It can be neither created nor destroyed. Instead, chi transforms itself and reappears in new states of existence. All states of existence, therefore, are temporary manifestations of chi, especially the states of physical matter.

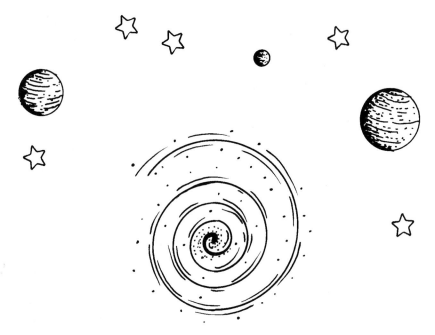

Fig. 1.1. Chi is the movement in the universe, but not the intelligence.

Chi is the source of all movement in the universe (fig. 1.1). The motions of the stars and planets, the radiation from the sun, and the patterns of our thoughts and emotions occur because of chi. It is considered to be the source of our life force and the animating factor in all living beings.

Chi also binds things together. It is what keeps the constituents of our bodies from separating and dissipating. When the human body loses its breath of life, the original energy (life force) leaves it, allowing the body to decompose.

Chi holds the organs, glands, blood vessels, and other bodily parts in place. When the body's chi becomes weak, a loosening of the organs can occur in which they drop from their normal positions, leading to poor functioning and ill health. Chi also warms the body; any increase or decrease in bodily heat indicates the strength of its flow. We think of warmth in mammals as a "vital sign," showing that chi is present.

The chi that forms Heaven and Earth is essentially the same as the chi that forms living beings. This was expressed by the ancient Chinese philosophers as follows:

Wu Chi (the Great Void) consists of chi. Chi condenses to become the myriad things. Things of necessity disintegrate and return to the Wu Chi. If chi condenses, its visibility becomes effective and physical form appears, chi in dispersion is substance, and so is it in condensation. Every birth is a condensation, every death a dispersal. Birth is not a gain, death not a loss. . . . When condensed, chi becomes a living being; when dispersed, it is the substratum of change.

—ZHANG TSAI (1020–1077 CE)

A human being results from the chi of Heaven and Earth. The union of the chi of Heaven and Earth is called human being (fig. 1.2).

—SIMPLE QUESTION, CHAPTER 25

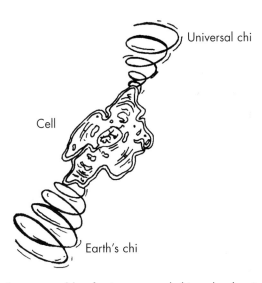

Fig. 1.2. Living cells are capable of using external chi to develop intelligence, contracting and creating as they build on themselves with more energy.

In *The Foundations of Chinese Medicine*, Giovanni Maciocia explains:

> According to the Chinese, there are many different "types" of human chi, ranging from the tenuous and rarefied, to the very dense and coarse. All the various types of chi, however, are ultimately one chi, merely manifesting in different forms.

The Bible's Book of Genesis says, "God created man in His image." Similarly, in Chinese thought, human beings are a microcosm of the universe. Thus, chi flows throughout the universe, and it also flows through humans. Through studying how our own chi works, we can also understand the workings of the universe. In Taoist Inner Alchemy, we begin the process of spiritual exploration within the laboratory of our own body and mind. The highest goal of Taoist Inner Alchemy is to transform our cells to unite with cosmic (higher self) energy and become immortal cosmic cells of the universe (fig. 1.3).

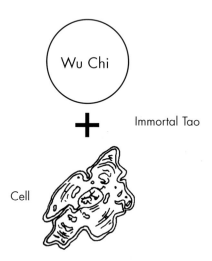

Fig. 1.3. The highest goal of Taoist Inner Alchemy is to transform our cells to unite with and become the cosmic cells of the universe. These cells are capable of living forever.

THE BEST INVESTMENT IS
YOUR OWN HEALTH

Many people put all their life force into earning money, until their vitalities are depleted and illnesses set in. They have to spend more and more of their money on hospitals, surgery, medicine, and, finally, spend most of their time in bed.

Many people say, "I don't have time to practice. My day is filled with appointments and work, meetings, study, and children." If you can improve your mind, body, and spiritual level of energy, your mind will be clearer; you will be more physically fit; your work will usually take less time to accomplish; and your emotions will be calmer.

Many students report the same problem: it is hard to find time to practice the Microcosmic Orbit meditation, Six Healing Sounds, Inner Smile, Tao Rejuvenation, Tai Chi Chi Kung, Iron Shirt, and Fusion of the Five Elements. It's true that it takes time to learn in the beginning; but after you learn it, it becomes a part of your life. For example, you can do the Inner Smile while waiting in line or sitting on a train. We spend a lot of time each day just waiting, and you can turn that time into practice time.

Many of our students study this system for a while and then find that they actually sleep less and eat less, so they end up having more time to do the practice. My knowledge and experience tell me that if people can put a thirty- to sixty-minute daily investment into their health each day, they will get one to four hours back and will be able to achieve more in less time. As a result, they will have more time to do more things.

TAOISM IN THE HOME

The Taoists do not regard differing characteristics or personal qualities of the husband and wife as the main sources of unhappiness in the family. It is natural for opposites to attract each other. The most important things are to understand each other, to look at each other's strong points, and to help to overcome each other's weak points.

In order to understand the other person, you have to understand yourself first. The best way to understand yourself is to get in touch with your own organs through the inner system and senses. You can then strengthen the organs in order to transform negative energy and cultivate positive emotions and values.

Negative emotions are the main causes of energy imbalances in the body. The existence of negative energy in one family member will create negative emotions in other family members and disturb the energy balance in the entire family.

Sexual Imbalances Can Be Modified with Practice

Another factor in the breakdown of the family is an imbalance in the sex life of the married couple. Healthy vitality is a major source of sexual energy. The organs and glands are the main source of sexual energy, and therefore, healthy organs and glands will increase the happiness of a couple's sex life. A stressful life, pollution, and the vast number of regulations that govern life in our society rob people of their organ and sexual energies. They are left depressed, with their vitality and sexual energy depleted. This leads to psychological and marital problems. These problems can cause muscular weaknesses, such as impotence (inadequate erection) in men and lack of muscle tone in the sexual organs of women. For a couple, the question is how to increase and transform their sexual energies and therefore correct the physiological problems of the sexual organs. In this book, we deal directly with strengthening the internal organs and senses.

The Peacefulness of Chi Energy

The balance of peaceful chi energy in a person is very important because it can help to balance the chi of another person who is close. Anything that is overly extreme will cause an imbalance of chi energy and will destroy peacefulness. There are five types of peace necessary in a family:

1. Peace of mind
2. Peace of the heart
3. Peace of the body
4. Peace of the organs
5. Peace of the senses

Taoism says that too much noise will hurt the ears and their associated organs, including the kidneys and the bladder, causing fear and disturbing the peace. Too much drinking or eating will hurt the spleen and, indirectly, the liver, which will result in anger and bad temper and will disturb the peace of the family. Too much watching television or movies will hurt the eyes, which will hurt the liver and the gallbladder and will cause a loss of energy, weakening the vitality of the entire body. Overexercising or overworking will hurt the tendons. Too much worry will hurt the nervous system.

Weakness of the organs or senses and nerves can cause certain types of unpleasant personal characteristics and bad habits, and these, in the long run, cause problems for the entire family. By understanding the sources of the problems and using the Inner Smile, the Six Healing Sounds, and the Tao Rejuvenation exercises and meditations together, family members can overcome the chi energy imbalance and organ weakness. It is important to understand the problems and to use the Taoist practices to help family members get over them, in order to avoid larger disturbances. By practicing together, the energies of the family members are exchanged and balanced together as a family unit. When one member of the family comes down with a sickness due to stress or negative emotional energy, other members of the family can help to balance that energy before further problems develop.

The Goals of the Universal Tao

The word *Tao* means the way—the way of nature and the universe, or the path of natural reality. It also refers to a way in which we can open our minds to learn more about the world, our spiritual paths, and ourselves.

A practical system. Taoism is a practice of body, mind, and spirit, not just a philosophy of mind. When we have the true sense of the Tao, of the real knowledge and wisdom, we will be able to make the right decisions in our lives.

Taoism involves many practical disciplines that can restore our lost youth, energy, and virtues while awakening our deepest spiritual potentials. Taoists regard these practices as a technology that can help us learn universal truths if we are willing to open our minds.

The final destiny. The ancient masters recognized that these potentials can include the possibility of attaining conscious freedom in the afterdeath state. Through specific exercises, we can avoid suffering the experience of death by expanding the consciousness beyond the physical body before its demise. This makes it possible to determine our future existence before leaving this life.

UNIVERSAL
SPIRITUAL INDEPENDENCE

All spiritual paths ultimately lead to the truth. The Tao is both a philosophy and a technology for seeking and finding the truths of the universe, nature, and humanity. Its focus goes beyond one single path or viewpoint. The Tao is not a religion, as it requires no initiations or ceremonies; but it is the outcome of all religions, departing from dogma at the point of truth. It leaves behind all religious beliefs, just as if they were the clothing of past seasons. The Tao is also the goal of science; but it leaves behind all scientific theories as partial and temporal descriptions of the integral truth. Taoism includes all matters of religion and science, yet its breadth goes far beyond the limits of devotion or intellect.

The master keys. Taoist teachings are like master keys unlocking all doors. They assist people in their lives, as do all religious teachings. Yet the teachings of the Tao transcend religion while retaining the essence of spirituality. They explain and demonstrate the truths of the universe directly, rather than on the level of emotions, thoughts, or beliefs. For this reason, students of the Tao have little cause for skepticism or endless searching.

The ultimate truth. Philosophy, science, and religions all contain some aspects of truth that reflect the Tao. The teachings of the Tao reflect the center of the ultimate truth (ourselves and the universe) and help us reach it on our own. We can believe in any religion or spiritual path and still benefit from these teachings, because the Tao serves only to promote universal spiritual independence. There are no ultimate masters or gurus in Taoism because we become our own masters, capable of controlling our own destinies and knowing who we really are as we explore the marvelous powers hidden within the Tao of humanity. All the great gods, immortals, sages, saints, and holy men and women are our teachers and advisers.

CULTIVATING BODY, MIND, AND SPIRIT

We need food to nourish our bodies, minds, and spirits. Religions try to fulfill us with spiritual food when we don't know how to fulfill ourselves. Taoism suggests that everything in life can provide nourishment for some aspect of our being if we know how to access that nourishment. Taoist practices can help us determine our goals and receive physical, mental, and spiritual food in a natural way. They also teach us how to return to our source, the Wu Chi (the Godhead), and thereby attain spiritual independence as we learn to live harmoniously with nature and the universe.

The practices of the Universal Tao have three main goals:

1. Learning to heal, love, and be kind to ourselves as we develop compassionate hearts and a wholeness of being.
2. Learning to help, heal, and love others from the abundance of healing and loving energies we receive from the forces of nature, Heaven, and Earth.
3. Learning about our Original Source and helping it unfold within ourselves.

THREE BODIES

The ancient Taoists saw the importance of working on all three levels of our being: the physical body, the energy body, and the spirit. All three are important in forming a ladder with which we may climb consciously into the spiritual worlds and, just as important, back into the physical world to be creatively active here. This ladder enables Taoists to learn about the inner worlds and to return to the physical world with knowledge and increased energy. An immortal body, which we develop in the practice of Internal Alchemy, enables us to establish a constant link between life and the afterdeath (or prebirth) state.

Ancient Taoist sages believed we were born to be immortal. We become mortal by draining ourselves of chi through engaging in excessive sexual activity, indulging in negative emotions, and depending only on material sources to supply our life force. The masters recognized that different levels of immortality can be achieved through Internal Alchemy, and they devised many practices for this purpose. The ability to transcend even death through the transmutation of one's physicality into the immortal spirit body is the highest goal of Taoism. This level, known as physical immortality, takes the longest to achieve.

Healing the Physical Body: Becoming Like a Child to Return to the Original Source

The basic foundation of Taoist practice is learning to conserve the physical energy within your body so that it will no longer scatter and weaken as a result of worldly interactions. Full spiritual independence requires that you avoid being drained of this energy through the eyes, ears, nose, and mouth, or through excessive sex. The novice in the Universal Tao system begins with a wide range of exercises that develop the physical body into an efficient and healthy organism, able to live in the world and yet stay free of the tensions and stresses of daily life. You aspire to return to a childlike state of innocence and vitality, to regain the original force that is your birthright. Specific goals of this level are to learn how to heal yourself, how to love yourself, and how to love others.

Foundation Practices: Conserving Energy to Follow the Light

The first level of practice is to develop a healthy body, which can take up to twelve months of diligent training. During this process we learn how to condense and conserve our life force through the Microcosmic Orbit meditation, the Healing Love practice, the Inner Smile, the Six Healing Sounds, and Iron Shirt Chi Kung. We learn to gather and refine our life force into a chi ball (energy sphere) so it will not dissipate when we are ready to leave this world. As people grow older, their life force weakens, often resulting in illness and suffering.

Using drugs to combat illness drains so much of the body's life force that we may not have enough energy left, at the moment of death, to follow the primordial light (clear light) to the Wu Chi (our Original Source—God). The basic practices of the Universal Tao ensure that we retain enough vital energy to make that journey.

Stopping energy leakage through conservation and recycling. The Microcosmic Orbit is the body's major energy pathway. Along this path there are nine openings. If we learn how to seal them when we are not using them, by that simple act of conservation we will immediately have more energy. Chapter 4 of this book gives a summary of the Microcosmic Orbit, but the basic Orbit is taught in great detail in my first book, *Awaken Healing Energy Through the Tao*. See also *Healing Light of the Tao*.

The Microcosmic Orbit meditation is the first step toward attaining the goals we have described, as it develops the power of the mind to control, conserve, recycle, transform, and direct chi (the Chinese term for energy, or life force) through the body's primary acupuncture channels. By managing our chi effectively, we gain better control over our lives; by using our energy wisely, we discover we already have plentiful chi.

With the advanced Microcosmic Orbit, we learn to connect with and draw from the unlimited source of universal love, a cosmic orgasm formed by the union of the three main sources of chi accessible to humans: the *universal force*, the *earth force*, and the *higher self (cosmic) force*. This process is both energizing and balancing. It prepares us for working with greater amounts of chi in the higher levels of meditative practice, particularly in developing the energy body.

Transforming negative energy into virtues: opening the heart. The Inner Smile and Six Healing Sounds are simple yet powerful practices that teach us how to relax and heal the vital organs and how to transform negative emotions back into a rich source of energy. They help open the heart center and connect us with unlimited universal love, improving daily interactions and providing a vehicle for the virtues, which derive from the internal organs. Taoists perceive the heart as the seat of love, joy, and happiness, through which we can connect with universal love. It is also a cauldron in which the energies of our virtues are combined and strengthened. Through practicing the Inner Smile, you will feel these virtuous energies generated from their respective organs. You will then gather these into the heart to be refined and blended into compassion, the highest of all virtues. This is a most effective way to enhance your best qualities.

Conserving, recycling, and transforming the sexual energy. A Taoist gains strength through the conservation and recycling of sexual energy, as described in my two books, *Taoist Secrets of Love* (for men) and *Healing Love Through the Tao* (for women). When collected, sexual energy (*ching chi*) becomes an incredible source of power that you can use individually or share with a sexual partner via the Microcosmic Orbit pathway during sexual intercourse. With practice, singles and couples can learn to increase and intensify sexual pleasure. The collected and transformed sexual energy is an important alchemical catalyst to use in higher meditations. Once you have abundant sexual energy, you can connect to the unlimited cosmic orgasm experienced every moment by your higher self, which is the most basic energy in every cell of your body.

Managing the life force. In the practices of Iron Shirt Chi Kung and Tai Chi Chi Kung, you learn to align the skeletal structure with gravity to allow a smooth, strong flow of energy. With strong fasciae, tendons, and bone marrow and good mechanical structure, you can manage your life force more efficiently. The body also gains a sense of being rooted deeply in the earth, so you can tap into the Mother Earth healing force.

Chi Nei Tsang. Chi Nei Tsang is the best technique for healing both yourself and other people without draining your own energies. Chi Nei Tsang is a Taoist abdominal massage system; it releases blockages that can prevent the smooth flow of energy in any of the bodily systems. These include the lymphatic, organ, meridian, circulatory, and nervous systems of the body.

Five-element nutrition. The Taoist approach to diet is based on determining the body's needs and then fulfilling them according to the five elements of nature, which support the five major organs of the body. This system reveals and strengthens any weak organs by balancing your food intake to enhance any deficient elements. It does not condemn most foods that people enjoy (including sweets), but instead creates a better program in which these foods can support the body's internal balance rather than disrupt it. Choosing and combining foods in this way can help us avoid the cravings we sometimes fall prey to.

Developing the Energy Body

Our Vehicle to Travel in Inner and Outer Space

The next level of the Universal Tao system consists of the Fusion of the Five Elements I, II, and III. These practices can take up to one or two years to learn well. They use the extra energy saved through the foundation practices, including recycled negative energies, to build a strong energy body that will not dissipate. Developing this energy body awakens a part of us that perceives and acts free of environmental, educational, and karmic conditioning. Once the energy body is strong, it becomes a vehicle (like the space shuttle) to help prepare the untrained soul and spirit for the long journey home, back to the Wu Chi.

At this stage of development, the energy body serves only as a vehicle, not yet having come to life through spiritual rebirth; but the energy body can still be trained to function in the heavenly realms.

If we do not have a chance to practice awakening or to give birth to the soul and immortal spirit during life, the primordial light will awaken us at the moment of death. Unfortunately, we may be too untrained and inexperienced to follow this light. To prepare for the journey, the energy body is a vehicle of great importance. We can train and educate the energy body so it can help the untrained soul and spirit recognize and follow the primordial light back to our Original Source.

It is also important during our lifetime to develop an "internal compass," which is associated with the pineal gland, to help us focus on the light when it comes to us.

When we are ready to give birth to the real soul, the energy body will act like a booster rocket to help boost the soul into its higher dimension of the immortal spirit. At the highest level, all three of these bodies merge into one.

Each level of development gives us a chance to go further in the journey back to the Wu Chi. Taoist methods of absorbing stellar energies help rejuvenate the physical body and strengthen the soul and spirit bodies for their interdimensional travels.

Recycling Our Negative Emotions

Our emotional life, filled with constant vicissitudes, drains our vital energy. Through the Fusion of the Five Elements meditations, we learn to transform into usable energy the sick energy of negative emotions that has become locked in the vital organs. Taoists understand morality and good deeds as the most direct path to self-healing and balance. Being good to others is good for the self as well. All the good energies we create are stored in the energy body like deposits in a bank account. By helping others and giving them love, kindness, and gentleness, we receive more positive energy back in return. When we open our hearts, we are filled with love, joy, and happiness. We can actually transform the essence of our hearts from the material into the immaterial to gather supplies of this positive energy for use in the heavens as well as on Earth.

From Taoist experience, we know that when we leave this world we can go directly to heaven, depending on how much energy we have been able to transform into the energy body prior to death. Just like money in the bank, the more we transform our physical being to our spiritual being, the more we have in heaven. The more good we do here, the more positive energy we have there.

Forming the Spirit Body

Planting the Seed of Immortality

The Inner Alchemy meditation of the Lesser Enlightenment of Kan and Li (water and fire, sex and love) reunites the male and female within each of us. It involves the practice of self-intercourse, which by internal sexual coupling of the sexual energies enables us to give birth to the soul body. The soul body then acts as a "babysitter" to help nurture the spirit body. The soul is the seed, but it can also be matured into the immortal body if we have not had the chance to raise the spirit body in this life. Practitioners of Taoist Alchemy believe that if we give birth to the spirit body and develop the immortal body in this life, we can overcome the cycle of reincarnation.

The newly formed babysitter or soul body is in the yin stage, or infancy; it is a soul embryo. We need to feed, raise, educate, and train the young soul to become fully grown.

Once we have developed the soul body, we can give birth to the spirit body. To cultivate the young spirit body until it is fully mature can take fourteen to eighteen years. At this stage we also use the energies of nature—trees, sun, moon, and stars; virtually all sensory experiences of a positive nature become nourishment for the growth of the spirit within the physical body.

Many masters who attained this level of the immortal body were able to transform the material into the immaterial and transfer it into the spirit body. At the moment of death, they were able to transfer their consciousness, their energy, and the physical elements of their bodies up with them into the spirit body, although even this level is not yet the true immortal body. In this process, their physical bodies actually shrank in size; after their physical deaths occurred, they may have weighed only two-thirds of their previous weight. This meant they had successfully transformed much of their material being into an immaterial state while retaining full consciousness.

Cultivating the Yang Stage of the Immortal Body:
Marrying the Light

We cannot breed a dog with a snake. To merge with the light of the Immortal Tao, we must awaken and nourish the awareness that we are in truth children of the light. Once we have fully grown the spirit body, it will be the same frequency as the light of the Tao and can become one with that light. Other traditions refer to this light by such names as the Holy Spirit or Great Spirit; we also refer to it as the outer light.

The Greater Kan and Li meditation teaches us how to recognize the inner light of our own spirits and shows us how to merge it with or "marry" it to the outer light. Once we capture and "marry the light," we give birth to the second stage of the true immortal spirit. Taoists refer to this as the yang body. We continue to transform the physical body energy to feed the immortal spirit so it can mature.

At this stage of practice, we learn to digest increasingly higher-grade energies of the higher self and universal forces from the sun, moon, planets, stars, and galaxies, and from the mind of the Tao itself. An awakening to that which is eternal and enduring occurs through this practice. Cognizant of our true nature as spirits, we experience the ability to leave the physical body and travel in the immortal spirit body, which leads to experience of the inner worlds of spirit. Fear of death is vanquished as we become familiar with life beyond physicality.

Greatest Enlightenment of Kan and Li

At this level we transfer all physical essence into the immortal body. When all the body's material elements are transformed into subtle chi, what remains is known as the rainbow body. When a master of this level leaves this world, there is nothing left of the physical body but nails and hair. Death is still necessary to speed up the process.

*Sealing of the Five Senses, Union of
the Kun and Kan, Reunion of Heaven and Man*

At this level the master transcends death entirely. He or she can simply transform the physical body into the immortal body and leave this world or return to it at will. This is the state of complete physical immortality. It takes from eighty to a few hundred years to master these practices and transform all the material elements of the body into the immaterial. At this stage the adept reaches the final goal of ascending to heaven in broad daylight.

There are records in Chinese history of many thousands of Taoist immortals who reached the level of daylight ascension in the presence of many witnesses. In the Bible, Elijah and Moses also accomplished this feat. In the final stage of this practice, we can unite the immortal spirit body, the energy body, and the physical body, or separate them at will. It is then that the human being knows full and complete freedom as an immortal, where no world is a boundary.

The Inner Smile Meditation

BENEFITS OF THE INNER SMILE

Low-Grade Energy or High-Grade Energy

In Taoism we regard the negative emotions as low-grade energy. Many people operate their lives in anger, sadness, depression, fear, worry, and other kinds of negative energy. These types of energy are bound to cause chronic disease and to steal our major life force. The Inner Smile is the true smile for all parts of the body, including all the organs, glands, and muscles, as well as the nervous system. It will produce a high grade of energy that can heal and eventually be transformed into an even higher grade of energy.

A genuine smile transmits loving energy, which has the power to warm and heal. Just recall a time when you were upset or physically ill and someone, perhaps a stranger, gave you a big smile—and suddenly you felt better. Norman Cousins, former editor of the *Saturday Review*, writes in *Anatomy of an Illness* that he cured himself of a rare connective tissue disease by watching old Marx Brothers movies. One of my students cured herself of cancer of the breast by continually practicing the Inner Smile to the part that was sick.

In ancient China, the Taoist masters recognized the power of smiling energy. They practiced an Inner Smile to themselves, which moved chi energy and produced a high grade of chi, and achieved health, happiness, and longevity. Smiling to oneself is like basking in love, and love can repair and rejuvenate (fig. 3.1).

The Inner Smile directs smiling energy into our organs and glands, which are so vital to life. Ironically, although we often pay a great deal of attention to our outer appearance, very few of us are aware of our inner organs and glands: what they look like, where they're located, or what their functions are. Worse yet, we are insensitive to the subtle warnings they send us when we mistreat them with poor diets and unhealthy lifestyles. We are like a boss who never pays any attention to his or her employees and is startled when things go wrong. If we're acquainted with our organs and glands, appreciate what they do, and learn to hear their messages, they will reward us with relaxation and vitality.

Honeylike Secretion or Poisonous Secretion

The Inner Smile is most effective in counteracting the stresses of life. In our current society, we spend millions of dollars just to find a way to relieve stress. Often, these remedies provide only partial and temporary relief.

The Inner Smile has a close relationship with the thymus gland and will increase the activity of that gland. In the Taoist system, the thymus gland is the seat of greater enlightenment, the seat of love, and the seat of the life-force chi energy. When we are under emotional stress, the thymus gland is the first to be affected. In his book *Your Body Doesn't Lie*, Dr. John Diamond presents a study that shows that the thymus has the role of the master controller that directs the life-giving and healing energies of the body. The theory of cancer formulated by Sir MacFarlane Burnet, the Australian Nobel Prize winner, suggests that increasing the thymus gland's activity will result in a greater ability to ward off cancer. One type of cells produced by the thymus is the T-cells. The function of the T-cells is to recognize abnormal cells and to destroy them. Of the billions of cells produced in the body each day,

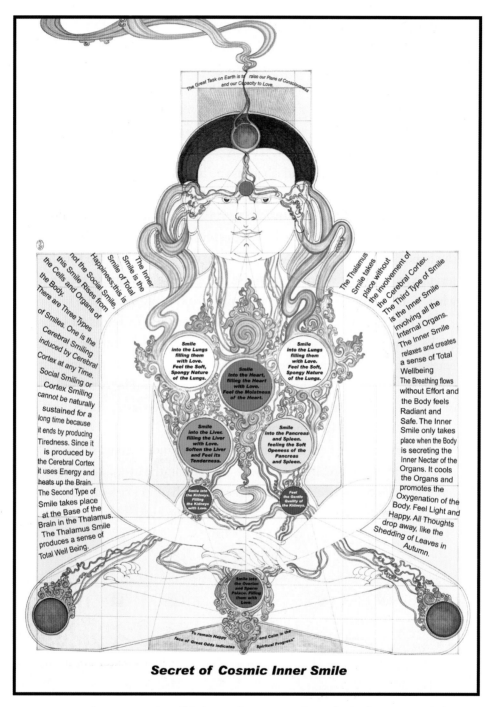

Secret of Cosmic Inner Smile

Fig. 3.1. The Inner Smile will help you have more chi and a higher grade of chi.

some will be abnormal. If the T-cells are not activated by the thymus hormone, the abnormal cells will continue to proliferate and develop into clinical cancer. Hence, the thymus gland plays a critical role in the prevention of cancer throughout adult life.

Applied Kinesiology gives a method to test the strength or weakness of the thymus gland, to which the Inner Smile will make an important difference. With a partner, try this test: Touch the thymus, located at the point where the second rib joins the breastbone below the throat. First have your partner not smile, but instead let the facial muscles drop and the corners of the mouth turn down. Have him or her keep one arm extended out to the side, resisting while you press down on the hand. Then, try it again with your partner smiling and see the difference in the resistive strength of the muscles. This demonstrates that when you smile, you activate the thymus gland (figs. 3.2 and 3.3).

Taoist sages say that when you smile, your organs release a honeylike secretion that nourishes the whole body. When you are angry, fearful, or under stress, they produce a poisonous secretion that blocks up the energy channels, settling in the organs and causing loss of appetite, indigestion, increased blood pressure, faster heart beat, insomnia, and negative emotions.

Smiling into your organs causes them to expand, become softer and moister and, therefore, more efficient. As a result, the liver, for example, has more room to store nutrients and detoxify harmful substances.

The practice of the Inner Smile begins in the eyes. They are linked

Fig. 3.2. The expression shown in this picture can decrease your energy level.

Fig. 3.3. The expression shown in this picture can increase your energy level.

to the autonomic nervous system, which regulates the action of the organs and glands. The eyes are the first to receive emotional signals and cause the organs and glands to accelerate at times of stress or danger (the fight-or-flight reaction) and to slow down when a crisis has passed. Ideally, the eyes maintain a calm and balanced level of response. Therefore, by simply relaxing your eyes, you can relax your whole body and thus free your energy for the activity at hand (see fig. 3.4).

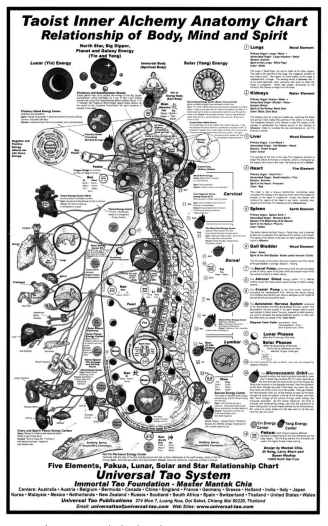

Fig. 3.4. The eyes are linked to the autonomic nervous system and can affect your level of energy.

Learning through the Inner Smile

In the Universal Tao system, we believe that our organs, our senses, and the various parts of our bodies are involved in learning. When you are stressed, overly emotional, or managing your life in anger or fear, your organs become obstructed and your performance levels are lowered. A lot of energy is eaten up, and you become dull, lacking alertness and playfulness. You are hindered in learning or developing new ideas, and if you try to force yourself to learn, the subject matter often will not remain in your mind and you will not be able to integrate it into yourself.

When you are stressed or fearful, all the organs and senses are closed. For example, when you do not like someone, your body does not want to accept the person and, thus, is not able to accept that person's teaching and ideas.

When you smile to your organs, senses, and glands, you make a connection and establish good communication with them. Then information can flow across the open lines of communication; you learn easily, find new ideas and new directions, and take on new endeavors with enthusiasm.

The Main Sources of Auditory Energy

The main sources of auditory energy are the kidneys and their associated organ, the bladder. When the kidneys are functioning well you will be more alert and, thus, able to learn. The kidneys are connected to the openings of the ears. The auditory sense—hearing —is very important in learning. When the kidneys are strong, you will increase your auditory sharpness, which will enhance your learning.

The bladder helps in eliminating toxic fluids, and this makes the blood cleaner and the fluids able to flow more freely. If the bladder is impaired, then the kidney functions will be affected.

The Main Sources of the Power of Speech

The main sources of speech power are the heart and its associated organ, the small intestine. The heart provides the spirit for learning and is the seat of joy. Without eagerness or a spirit to learn, learning will be difficult. The secret of learning is joyfulness, fun, and delight. When these are present your whole body will accept what you learn into itself. The heart is also the seat of respect and honesty. When you have respect, your heart is open. The tongue connects to the heart, and when that connection is open, you can start to accept and program your mind in bits and pieces, assimilating and putting into order what you have learned.

Many times, in order to learn new things, we need time to assimilate them into our systems. The small intestine helps you assimilate. When the small intestine has a problem, it impedes assimilation, and it also affects the heart's functions.

The Main Sources of Visual Energy

The main sources of visual energy are the liver and its associated organ, the gallbladder. When the liver is in good working order, you will be able to be more assertive, more decisive, and more able to integrate the things you learn. The opening for the liver is the eyes. When the liver is weak or sick, or you are angry or under stress, you'll be unable to make decisions and your vision will be impaired, making it difficult to program into your mind what you see and to integrate what you learn. A healthy gallbladder helps you make decisions more easily, too.

The Main Sources of Gestational Energy

The main sources of gestational energy are the spleen and the stomach. The spleen gives the good sense of inclusiveness. It is the opening for the mouth and is involved with the sense of taste and with digesting what you learn.

The spleen's associated organ is the stomach. When the stomach is in good condition, you will be more receptive to new thoughts, new ideas, and new ways. Once you have accepted these as your own, you will be even more willing to learn new things and more economic ways of doing them.

The Main Sources of Olfactory and Kinesthetic Energies

The main sources of olfactory and kinesthetic energies are the lungs and the large intestine. The lungs are associated with good impulses, and their openings are the nose and skin. They are involved with kinesthetic feeling—the sense of touch and feeling and the senses of the skin—thereby increasing your awareness of your surroundings and, thus, tremendously increasing your ability to learn.

The large intestine is involved in elimination and release and makes you more open, physically and mentally. When you are constipated, you are more closed, not open to new ideas and not willing to change. Even though only a small step might be required to change, some students will not let go of old ways or ideas to succeed. The large intestine is the associate organ of the lungs and helps strengthen the lungs' functions.

The Energy of the Sexual Organs Increases Creative Power

The sexual organs are the seat of energy for creative power. When you have low sexual energy, you will be less creative and will be stuck in old, inefficient ways. When you know how to smile to increase your sexual energy, you will increase your power to solve problems in daily life. At the same time, you will augment your originality and innovation in any creative projects you devote yourself to.

The Energy of the Adrenal Glands Gives You Enthusiasm to Learn

The adrenal glands give you vitality and the hot energy, or yang energy, of the kidneys. This yang energy peps you up and makes you enthusiastic to learn. If the adrenals are not active and healthy, without that vitality you will feel lazy and sleepy; you will have little eagerness for learning.

The Thyroid and Parathyroid Glands
Help the Power of Expression

The thyroid and parathyroid glands are intimately connected with communication. Having a smiling energy connection with these glands will help you increase your ability to express your opinions and your experiences so that all the senses can be involved in learning.

The Thymus Gland Helps the Immune System

The thymus gland is the seat of energy, and it helps you in strengthening your immune system. The thymus creates energy in the form of enthusiasm and in this way gives you strength and energy to learn.

The Spine Is the Center of Communication

The spine is the center of control and the center of communication. Know how to smile down into your spine and relax it, and you will increase your communication powers; you will know how to communicate what you have learned through your spine into your organs, and you will be able to accept new and more efficient ways into your system. The spine is also known as the controller of the networks.

Five Guidelines for Super Learning

1. Smile throughout learning. Smile to the parts or organs that are resistant to new ideas. For example, if the heart is unwilling to be accepting and open, smile to it to release the joys and fun of learning. If the liver has too much anger, which shuts off vision, smile to it until it is open.
2. Let your hands, legs, head, chest, eyes, nose, mouth, ears, tongue, anus, in fact any body part, all be involved in learning by acting things out. For example, if you are learning how to work on a new computer, let yourself act or imagine that you are the computer. Get inside and understand it; use your hands, eyes, ears, and so forth, and let them all be in contact with what you want to learn.

3. Smile to the senses and let them all open and feel light and happy to learn. Let them all be involved in learning. Start from vision; go through the auditory, olfactory, kinesthetic, and gustatory senses. Imagine or involve what you are going to learn with your visual sense of what it looks like, with your auditory sense of how it will sound, with your olfactory sense of how it will smell, with your kinesthetic sense of how it will feel, and with your gustatory sense of how it will taste.

4. Use the metaphors of your daily life that you know or use the most. For example, if you are a gardener or a lover of flowers, you can connect the things you are learning with what you know about gardening or flowers. Or if you are an animal lover, you can transform the things you learn into animals and metaphors about characteristics that are like the animals' characteristics.

5. Involve your total self in learning. Check out your whole system—your senses, your organs, your arms, your hands, and so on. All the parts of you can be willing to learn, so it is useful to recognize what they don't want to learn. When you open up the connection through the Inner Smile, you may identify the causes of resistance in parts of your body; smile to them; tell them you love them and want them to get involved.

Personal Power through the Inner Smile

The smile is the most powerful energy of personal power. The true inner smile from your organs will make all the organs contribute their own power to generate and stream out to your senses, especially your eyes. The eyes connect to all the organs and senses. Once you know how, you can get power to and from all the organs.

Imagine: We have sixty-three trillion cells in our bodies. Each cell gives out a very small amount of energy. Multiplied by sixty-three trillion cells, the energy is tremendous. When you are relaxed and calm, and you smile, you can maintain energy at its peak performance and always be ready to take action. The level of energy is always the main clue.

When your level of energy increases, you will have more energy to increase your skills, you will have more flexibility of action, and you will know better what you want and how to get it—that is, you will have specificity.

Make sure to smile to the sexual organs. The higher the level of sexual energy that you have, the more personal power you will have. When sexual power decreases, personal power decreases, too. Practice how to conserve and increase sexual energy by recycling it. Foods or drugs that claim to increase sexual power are not going to last long, if at all, and they cannot increase energy or be effective in the long run. Knowledge of how to cultivate sexual energy is one of the main sources of power.

PREPARATION FOR THE INNER SMILE

Wait at least an hour after eating to begin the practice, and choose a quiet spot in which to practice. It might help in the beginning to disconnect the phone. Later on, you will be able to practice almost anywhere with any noise, but for now you need to eliminate distractions in order to develop your inner focus.

Dress warmly enough so as not to be chilled. Wear loose-fitting clothes, and loosen your belt. If your environment is very warm, you can practice with little or no clothing on to eliminate any constriction and enhance the flow of information to and from the organs and senses. Remove your glasses and watch.

1. Sit comfortably on your sitz bones at the edge of a chair (fig. 3.5). The genitals should be unsupported because they are an important energy center. This means if you are a man, the scrotal sac hangs free of the edge of the chair. If you are a woman practicing without clothing on, you should cover your genitals with cloth to ensure no energy loss through them.

2. The legs should be hip width apart, and the feet should be solidly on the floor.

3. Sit comfortably erect with your shoulders relaxed and your chin slightly in.

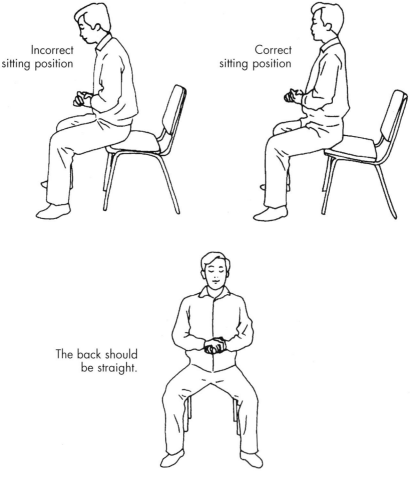

Incorrect sitting position

Correct sitting position

The back should be straight.

Fig. 3.5. Sitting posture

4. Place your hands comfortably on your lap, the right palm on top of the left (fig. 3.6). You may find it easier for the back and shoulders if you raise the level of your hands by placing a pillow under them.

5. Breathe normally. Close your eyes. While concentrating, the breath should be soft, long, and smooth. After a while you can forget about your breath. Attention to breath will only distract the mind, which must focus on drawing energy to the desired points. There are thousands of esoteric breathing methods; you might spend your whole life mastering them and acquire no lasting energy.

6. Position of the tongue: The tongue is the bridge between the two major energy channels. Its function is to govern and connect the energies of the thymus gland and pituitary gland, and it can balance the left and right brain energies. There are three positions for the tongue. At the beginning, place the tongue where it is most comfortable. If it is uncomfortable to place the tongue on the palate, place it near the teeth (fig. 3.7).

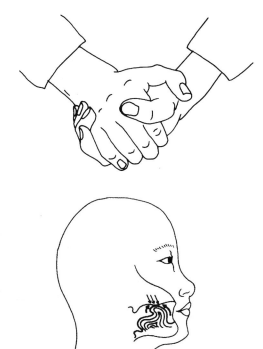

Fig. 3.6. Close the circuits in the hands, with the left hand on the bottom and the right hand on the top.

Fig. 3.7. Tongue position

The Inner Smile Practice

 ### Smiling Down to the Organs—the Front Line

1. Relax your forehead. Begin the Inner Smile by picturing a radiant, smiling face in front of you, ideally the face of someone you love. Or imagine seeing a beautiful sight, one that would make you smile. Allow the bliss of that love and beauty to enter your forehead and expand into a pleasurable glow, soothing away the tension and strain you may be holding around your eyes. Feel that smiling energy, in your eyes.

2. Allow that smiling energy to flow to the midpoint between your eyebrows (fig. 3.8). Let it flow into the nose, then the cheeks.

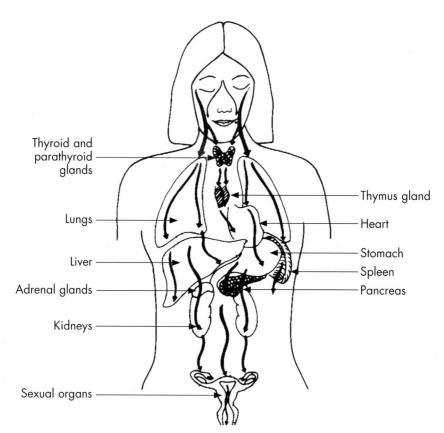

Fig. 3.8. Front line smile: major vital organs

Feel it relaxing the facial skin, then going deep inside the face muscles; feel it warming your whole face like sunshine. Let it flow into the mouth and slightly lift up the corners of the mouth. Let it flow into the tongue. Float the tip of the tongue. Then put your tongue up to the roof of the mouth and leave it there for the rest of the practice; this connects the two major channels of energy, the Governor and the Functional. Bring the smiling energy to the jaw. Feel the jaw releasing the tension that you commonly hold there.

3. Smile into your neck and throat, also common areas of tension. Although the neck is narrow, it is a major thoroughfare for most of the systems of the body. Air, food, blood, hormones, and signals from the nervous system all travel up and down the neck (fig. 3.9). When we are stressed, the systems are overworked; the neck is jammed with activity, and we get a stiff neck. Be like the Taoist masters and think of your neck as a turtle's neck—let it sink down into its shell and let it rest from the burden of holding up your heavy head (fig. 3.10). Smile into your neck and feel the energy opening your throat and melting away the tension.

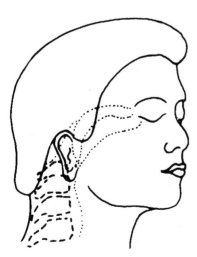

Fig. 3.9. The neck is a major thoroughfare for most of the body's systems.

Fig. 3.10. Think of your neck as a turtle's neck and let it sink down and rest.

4. Smile into the front part of your neck, the throat, where the thyroid and parathyroid glands are. This is the seat of your power to speak, and when it is stuck, the chi cannot flow. When it is tense and held back, you cannot express yourself. You will be cowardly in your interactions and frightened in front of a crowd, and your communications will break down. Smile down to the thyroid gland and feel the throat open, like a flower blossom (fig. 3.11).

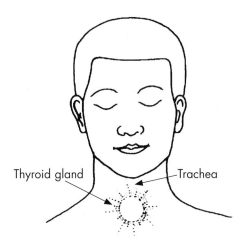

Thyroid gland   Trachea

Fig. 3.11. The throat is the seat of
your power to speak.

5. Let the energy of the smile flow down to the thymus gland, the seat of fire, the seat of chi, and the seat of healing energy. Smile down into it, feel it start to soften and moisten. Feel it grow bigger, like a flower bulb, and gradually blossom. Feel the fragrance of warm energy and healing chi flow out and down to the heart (fig. 3.12).

6. Let the smiling energy flow into your heart, which is the size of a fist and is located a little to the left of the center of the chest. The heart is the seat of love, the seat of compassion, the seat of honest respect, and the seat of joy. Feel the heart, like a bulb, gradually blossom and send the fragrant warmth of chi love, joy, and compassion radiating throughout all the organs from the pumping of

the heart. Let the smile energy fill your heart with joy. Thank your heart for its constant and essential work in pumping blood at the right pressure to circulate throughout your body. Feel it open and relax as it works more easily (fig. 3.13).

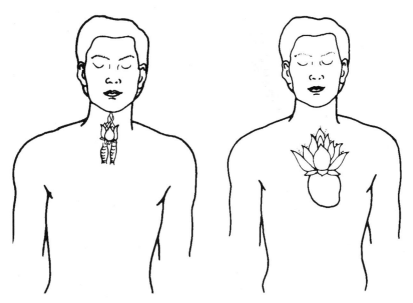

Fig. 3.12. Feel the thymus gland gradually blossom.

Fig. 3.13. The heart is the seat of joy; feel it gradually open like a bulb.

7. Bring the smiling and joyful energy from the heart to the lungs. Smile into every cell of your lungs. Thank your lungs for their wonderful work in supplying oxygen to the body and releasing carbon dioxide. Feel them soften and become spongier, moister. Feel them tingling with energy.

    Smile into the lungs deep inside and smile your sadness and depression away. Fill the lungs with the fragrance of righteousness that is induced by the love, compassion, and joy from the heart. Let the smile energy of joy, love, and righteousness flow down to the liver.

8. Smile into your liver, the large organ located mainly on the right side at the bottom of the rib cage. Thank it for its marvelously complex part in digestion—processing, storing, and releasing

nutrients—and its work in detoxifying harmful substances. Feel it soften and grow moister.

Refresh the smiling energy and get deep into the liver. See any anger and hot temper lying in the liver. Smile them away; let the joyfulness, loveliness, righteousness, and warmth of the chi induce the nature of the liver—kindness—to flow, until it is full and overflows out to the kidneys and adrenal glands.

9. Bring the smiling energy into your kidneys, just inside the lower part of your rib cage in the back on either side of the spine. Thank the kidneys for their work in filtering the blood, excreting waste products, and maintaining water balance. Feel them grow cooler, fresher, and cleaner. Smile into your adrenals, on top of your kidneys. Thank the adrenals for their contribution; they produce adrenaline for fight-or-flight situations and several other hormones. Your adrenals may return the thanks by giving you a little extra shot of energy.

    Refresh your smile again and get deep into the kidneys. See and feel if there is any fear lying inside the kidneys. Smile with the warmth of joy, love, and kindness, and melt your fears away. Let the nature of the kidneys—gentleness—come out and fill them until they overflow to the pancreas and spleen.

10. Smile into your pancreas and spleen. First smile into your pancreas, which is located at the center and to the left at and above waist level. Thank it for producing enzymes for digestion and insulin for regulating your blood sugar level. Then smile to the spleen, which is toward the bottom and left side of the rib cage. Thank it for producing antibodies against certain diseases. Feel it grow softer and fuller.

    Smile again into the spleen and pancreas; feel and see deep inside if there is any worry hidden; let the warmth of joy, love, righteousness, kindness, and gentleness melt your worries away. Smile into the virtue of the spleen—fairness. Bring it out and let it grow downward to the bladder and sexual region.

11. Bring the smiling energy down to the genital area in the lower

abdomen. For women, this is called the Ovary Palace and is located about three inches below the navel, midway between the ovaries. Smile into the ovaries, the uterus, and the vagina.

For men, this is called the Sperm Palace and is located one and a half inches above the base of the penis, in the area of the prostate gland and seminal vesicles. Smile down to the prostate gland and the testicles. Thank them for making hormones and giving you sexual energy.

Let love, joy, kindness, and gentleness flow into the genital organs so you can have power to overcome and eliminate uncontrollable sexual desires. You are the one who controls your sex drive; it does not control you. Thank your genitals for their work in making you the gender that you are. Sexual energy is the basic energy of life.

12. Return your attention to your eyes again. Quickly smile down into all the organs in the front line, checking each one for any remaining tension. Smile into the tension until it is released.

🌀 Smiling Down the Digestive System— the Middle Line

1. Become aware once more of the smiling energy in your eyes. Let it flow down to your mouth (see fig. 3.14 on page 42). Become aware of your tongue, and make some saliva by working your mouth and swishing your tongue around. Put the tip of your tongue to the roof of the mouth, tighten the neck muscles, and swallow the saliva hard and quickly, making a gulping sound as you do. With your inner smile, follow the saliva down the esophagus to your stomach, located at the bottom of the esophagus and below the heart toward the left side of the rib cage. Thank it for its important work in liquefying and digesting your food. Feel it grow calm and comfortable. Sometimes we abuse our stomachs with improper food. Make a promise to your stomach that you will give it good food to digest.

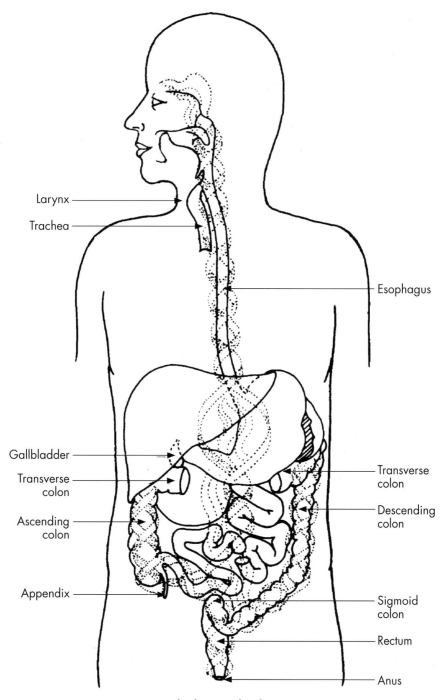

Fig. 3.14. Smile down to the digestive system.

2. Smile into your small intestine: the duodenum, the jejunum, and the ileum, in the middle of the abdomen. The small intestine is about seven meters long in an adult. Thank it for absorbing food nutrients to keep you vital and healthy.

3. Smile into your large intestine: the ascending colon, starting at the right side of the hip bone and passing upward to the undersurface of the right lobe of the liver; the transverse colon, which passes from the right liver region across the abdomen to the left beneath the lower end of the spleen; the descending colon, which passes downward through the left side of the lumbar region; and the sigmoid colon, which normally lies within the pelvis, the rectum, and the anus. The large intestine is about one and a half meters long. Thank it for eliminating wastes and for making you feel clean, fresh, and open. Smile to it and feel it be warm, nice, clean, comfortable, and calm.

4. Return attention to your eyes. Quickly smile down the middle line, checking for tension. Smile into the tension until it melts away.

Smiling Down the Spine—the Back Line

1. Bring your attention back to the smiling energy in your eyes again.

2. Smile inward with the eyes; collect the power of the smile in the third eye (mid-eyebrow). With your inner eyesight, direct your smile about three to four inches inward, into your pituitary gland, and feel the gland blossom. Direct the smile with your eyes into the third ventricle (the Third Room, the power room of the nervous system, highly magnified), the small cavity deep in the center of your brain. Feel the room expand and grow with bright, golden light, shining throughout your brain. Smile into the thalamus, from where the truth and power of the smile will generate. Smile into the pineal gland behind the thalamus and

feel this tiny gland gradually swell and grow like a flowering bulb. Move your smile's eyesight, like a bright, shining light, up to the left side of the brain. Move the inner smiling eyesight back and forth, in the left brain and cerebellum and across the corpus callosum into the right brain and cerebellum. This will balance the left and right brain and strengthen the nerves (figs. 3.15, 3.16, and 3.17).

3. Move the inner smiling eyesight down to the midbrain; feel it expand and soften. Feel the smiling energy go down the brain stem to the pons and medulla oblongata (see fig. 3.16) and into the spinal

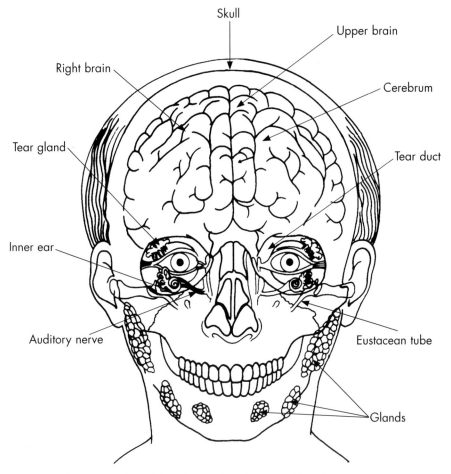

Fig. 3.15. Parts of the brain and head

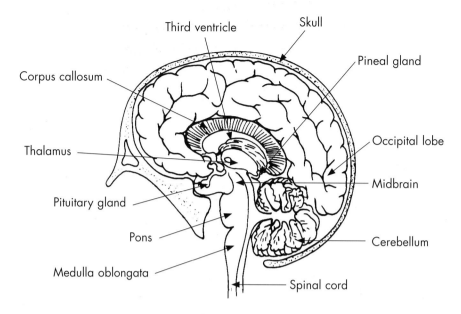

Fig. 3.16. Side view cross section of the brain

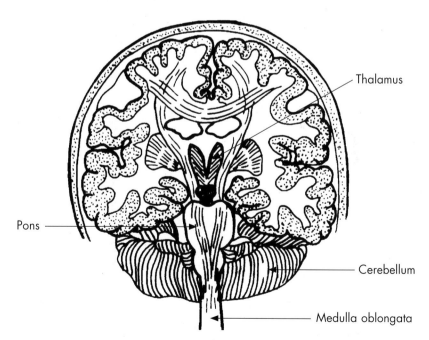

Fig. 3.17. Transverse vertical cross section of the brain

cord. Starting from the cervical vertebra at the base of the skull, move the inner smiling eyesight down along the spinal cord and into the spinal column protecting it. Bring the loving energy down the spinal column, into each vertebra and the disc below it (fig 3.18). Count out each vertebra and disc as you smile down the vertebrae: seven cervical (neck) vertebrae, twelve thoracic (chest) vertebrae, five lumbar (lower back) vertebrae, the triangular bone called the sacrum, and the coccyx (tailbone). Feel the spinal cord and the back becoming loose and comfortable. Feel the vertebrae

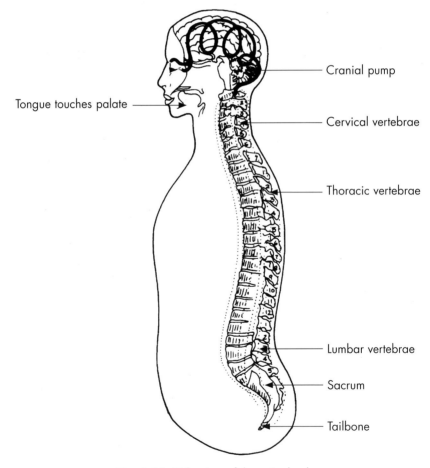

Fig. 3.18. Side view of the spinal column

relaxing and the discs of the spinal column softening. Feel your spine expanding and elongating, making you taller.

4. Return to your eyes and quickly smile down the entire back line. Your whole body should feel relaxed; the Back Line exercise increases the flow of the spinal fluid and sedates the nervous system. And smiling into the discs of the spinal column keeps them from hardening and becoming deformed so they can no longer absorb the force and weight of the body. Smiling into the spine can prevent or relieve back pain.

Smiling Down the Entire Length of Your Body

1. Start at the eyes again, and refresh the loving, soothing smile energy there. Direct your inner smile's eyesight. Quickly smile down the front line. Follow the smiling down the middle line, and then down the back line. When you are more experienced, smile down all three lines simultaneously, being aware of the organs and the spine.
2. Now, feel the energy descend down the entire length of your body, like a waterfall—a waterfall of smiles, joy, and love. Feel your whole body being loved and appreciated. How marvelous it is!

Collecting the Smiling Energy at the Navel

It's very important to end by storing the smiling energy in the navel. Most ill effects of meditation are caused by excess energy in the head or heart. The navel area can safely handle the increased energy generated by the Inner Smile practice.

1. To collect the smile's energy, concentrate on gathering the energy in your navel area, which is about one and a half inches inside your body.
2. Now, mentally move that energy in an outward spiral around your navel 36 times; don't go above the diaphragm or below the pubic

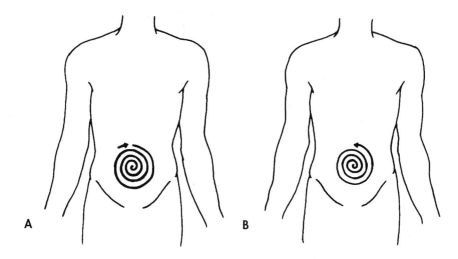

(A) Collect the energy in the navel, and circle it 36 times clockwise.
(B) Circle the energy 24 times counterclockwise.

Fig. 3.19. Collecting smiling energy in the navel for men

bone. Men, start the spiral clockwise (fig. 3.19). Women, start the spiral counterclockwise (fig. 3.20). Use your finger as a guide the first few times.

3. Next, reverse the direction of the spiral and bring it back into the navel, circling it 24 times. Again, use your finger as a guide the first few times.

The energy is now safely stored in your navel, available to you whenever you need it and for whatever part of your body needs it. You have now completed the Inner Smile.

Daily Use

Try to practice the Inner Smile every day as soon as you wake up. It will improve your whole day. If you love your own body, loving becomes a habit; you will be more loving to others and more effective in your work. Once you have learned the technique and have practiced it regularly you can, if you are short of time, do it more rapidly, in a few minutes.

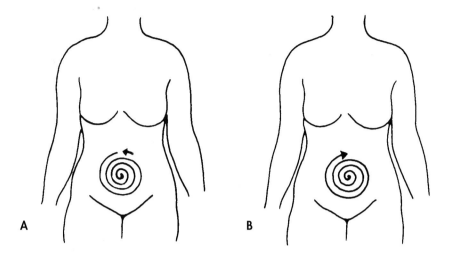

(A) Collect the energy in the navel, and circle it 36 times counterclockwise.

(B) Circle the energy 24 times clockwise.

Fig. 3.20. Collecting smiling energy in the navel for women

Smile the Negative Emotions Away

Practice the Inner Smile also at times of stress, anger, fear, impatience, or depression. Smile down into the part that feels tension and strain, and gradually see the negative energy transform into positive vital life-force energy. These draining, negative emotions will be turned into positive energy and vitality. Smile the emotions away. The smile's energy can change emotional energy into vital energy—provided you smile enough into the emotions.

Smile Pain and Sickness Away

If you feel pain and uneasiness in any part of your body, or feel sick in any part of the organs, keep on smiling to these parts. Spend more time smiling to these parts, and open up the lines of communication. Talk to them, get feedback from them, stay engaged until you feel them get softer or more open or their color changes from dark to bright.

4

The Microcosmic
Orbit Meditation

The Inner Smile, the Six Healing Sounds, and the Tao Rejuvenation practices will gradually increase your life-force energy by transforming stress into vitality. To use this energy efficiently and safely for further healing and growth, you must circulate it through specific pathways in your body.

It is much easier to cultivate your energy if you first understand the major paths of energy circulation in the body. The nervous system in humans is very complex and is capable of directing energy wherever it is needed. The ancient Taoist masters discovered that there are two energy channels that carry an especially strong current.

One channel is called the Functional or Yin Channel. It begins at the base of the trunk, midway between a man's testicles or a woman's vagina and the anus, at a point called the perineum. It goes up the front of the body past the sex organs, digestive organs, heart, and throat, and ends at the tip of the tongue. The second channel, called the Governor or Yang Channel, starts in the same place but goes up the back of the body. It flows from the perineum upward into the tailbone and then up through the spine into the brain and back down to the roof of the mouth.

The tongue is like a switch that connects these two currents—when you touch it to the roof of the mouth just behind the front teeth, your energy can flow in an unbroken current up the spine and back down the front of the body, forming a single circuit called the Microcosmic Orbit (see fig. 4.1 on page 52). This vital current circulates past the major organs and nerve systems of the body, giving cells the juice they need to grow, heal, and function. This circulating energy forms the basis of acupuncture. Western medical research has already acknowledged acupuncture as being clinically effective, although scientists admit they cannot explain why the system works. The Taoists, on the other hand, have been studying the subtle energy points in the body for thousands of years and have verified in detail the importance of each channel.

It is this loop of energy about the body that also carries the organ energy and smiling energy and spreads vitality to other parts of the body. By opening up this microcosmic channel and keeping it clear of physical or mental blockages, it is possible to pump the life-force energy up the spine. If this channel is blocked by tension, then learning to circulate the Microcosmic Orbit is an important step to opening up the blockages in the body, so as to nourish and revitalize all parts of the mind and body. Otherwise, when intense pressure builds in the head, much of it escapes out the eyes, ears, nose, and mouth and is lost. This is like trying to heat a room while all the windows are open—you're going to have a very high fuel bill.

Circulating Your Chi in the Microcosmic Orbit

The way to open this microcosmic energy channel is by sitting in meditation for a few minutes each morning after you do the Inner Smile. Touch your tongue to the roof of your mouth. Allow your energy to complete the loop by letting your mind flow along with it. Start in the eyes, and mentally circulate with the energy as it goes down the front through your tongue, throat, chest, and navel, to the perineum, and then up the tailbone and spine to the head (fig. 4.1).

At first it will feel like nothing is happening, but eventually the current will begin to feel warm in some places as it loops around. The

Functional Channel

Governor Channel

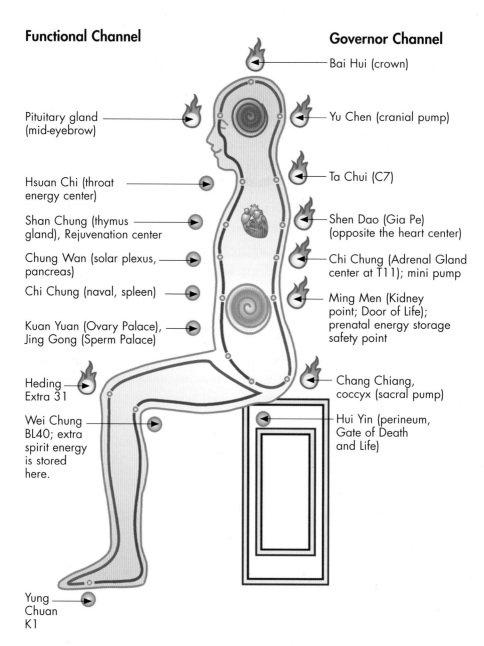

Bai Hui (crown)

Pituitary gland (mid-eyebrow)

Yu Chen (cranial pump)

Hsuan Chi (throat energy center)

Ta Chui (C7)

Shan Chung (thymus gland), Rejuvenation center

Shen Dao (Gia Pe) (opposite the heart center)

Chung Wan (solar plexus, pancreas)

Chi Chung (Adrenal Gland center at T11); mini pump

Chi Chung (naval, spleen)

Ming Men (Kidney point; Door of Life); prenatal energy storage safety point

Kuan Yuan (Ovary Palace), Jing Gong (Sperm Palace)

Heding Extra 31

Chang Chiang, coccyx (sacral pump)

Wei Chung BL40; extra spirit energy is stored here.

Hui Yin (perineum, Gate of Death and Life)

Yung Chuan K1

Fig. 4.1. Learn to circulate your chi in the Microcosmic Orbit to assist in counteracting stress. The tongue touches the roof of the palate to complete the circuit of the Governor and Functional Channels.

key is simply to relax and try to bring your mind directly into the part of the loop you are focusing on. This is different from visualizing an image inside your head of what that part of the body looks like or is feeling. Do not use your mind as if it were a television picture. Experience the actual chi flow. Relax and let your mind flow with the chi in the physical body along a natural circuit to any desired point, such as your navel, perineum, and so forth.

Study of the Microcosmic Orbit is highly recommended to all students who want to become skilled in transforming stress and who seek to truly master the techniques of the Universal Tao. Without first learning the Microcosmic Orbit, progress to the higher levels of transforming emotional energy is very difficult. Some people may already be open in these channels or relaxed when they are close to nature. The benefits of the Microcosmic Orbit extend beyond the obvious result of facilitating the flow of life-force energy and include prevention of aging and the healing of many ailments and illnesses, ranging from arthritis to high blood pressure, insomnia, and headaches. To learn more about the Microcosmic Orbit, see my book *Healing Light of the Tao: Foundational Practices to Awaken Chi Energy.*

The Virtues and Transforming Stress

The Heart of the Universal Tao Practices

The quality of our internal energy is just as important to our health and spiritual development as the quantity. As we increase our internal energy flow and accumulate a surplus of chi, we must emphasize spiritual development to maintain balance in our daily lives. In essence, our spiritual qualities are our positive attributes, or what the Taoists call *virtues*. Our virtues have the nature of wisdom and love. They are wise because they reflect our interdependence with the Tao, with nature, with all life, and with the different parts of our own body. We cannot exhibit the virtues except in relation to each other. The virtues are also wise because they express love: the attitude that strengthens the positive bonds connecting everything in the universe.

We need food to sustain our lives. Physically, we need material food; but we also must nourish other, subtler bodies within us. These are the soul and spirit bodies. The energy of our virtues, the universe, the stars, and the planets provide a source of spiritual food. Although we are trained to depend on our religious beliefs to give us this nourishment, spiritual food is actually all around us. We need to learn how to absorb and digest it. The Universal Tao offers the means by which we can access these nurturing energies, to cultivate the soul and spirit and to enhance our total being.

Taoism recognizes that both the development of the virtues' energies, and the cultivation of life force to create the soul and spirit bodies, are important aspects of spiritual growth. These approaches are related, because as we retain and recycle internal energy into life force, this abundance of chi helps us to open and still our minds/hearts, and this brings forth inner joy, happiness, and love and other virtues. When combined, all these give birth to the subtler bodies of energy and spirit.

Taoists believe that we are born with the virtue qualities of love, gentleness, kindness, respect, honesty, fairness, justice, and righteousness. When we are abundant with these virtues, our life force flows smoothly and efficiently. If we neglect to cultivate the virtues, however, we run the risk of channeling our accumulated energies directly into our negative emotions, amplifying any negative or neurotic tendencies we may have.

Actually, there is nothing wrong with these negative emotions as long as we recognize them and know how to transform them, so they will not block the energy in the organs. It is necessary to find a balance and to learn to acknowledge the totality of ourselves, both the light and the dark sides.

Our society is known for its fast pace, its stressful conditions, and its inability to handle the tons of garbage it produces daily. This includes not only the trash from people's homes, but also the emotional garbage produced within their bodies. Under the influence of this stressful society, their virtues gradually diminish, and negative emotions such as anger, fear, worry, and impatience arise. These further weaken the virtues, gradually forcing people to survive on low-grade, negative energies. The symptoms manifest, at their extremes, as disease, social disorders, and violence.

To regain the virtues, we must first become aware of and transform our negative emotions into useful energy. Normally, we throw these emotions out like garbage, thereby polluting each other and society with useless wasted energy. Like garbage, negative emotions can cause a great deal of damage to both our internal and external environment.

Just as we can transform garbage into compost and use it as fertilizer for our gardens, we can transform negative emotions, which will always come up, into the fertile ground for growing our positive virtues (fig. 5.1). If we don't compost, these emotions will have harmful

Hate into love

Sadness and depression into courage

Anger into kindness

Fear into gentleness

Worry into openness

Fig. 5.1. Transform negative energy into positive energy.

effects on the internal organs and glands and may drain our life force, causing our bodies to function on less energy and at a lower vibration. Medical science acknowledges that the presence of negative emotions can wear down the body's resistance before any clinical evidence of disease exists.

Taoists believe that emotions originate in the organs (fig. 5.2). Once you can differentiate between and become aware of the different kinds of emotional energy that reside in the organs, you can deal with them more easily. You must observe what outside influences trigger their appearance. This means noticing, for example, how another person's negative emotion triggers anger or sadness in you. Once you have this awareness, you can transfer these emotions into positive life

Fig. 5.2. Connect the organs and their elements.

force for yourself. Don't permit them to accumulate in your organs as negative emotional energy to trouble you. By building up a lot of positive life force, you will be able to transform your own "garbage" energy better.

COMPASSION: THE HIGHEST VIRTUE

Compassion is the highest virtue and the most useful energy to share with others. It is the fusion of all the virtues together into their purest expression. To attain compassion, you must first recycle negative emotional energies to restore and increase the life force. This, in turn, will nourish the positive energies of the organs so that each organ can produce its respective virtue in abundance. You can channel a surplus of virtue energy for the benefit of other people. If you try to practice compassion without transforming the negative emotions and reestablishing the virtue energies, you will have little to offer anyone.

Compassion is the supreme expression of human emotion and virtuous energy. It is the most beneficial energy to share with others. It signifies a level of development that takes hard work and serious meditation before it can blossom in your life. It is not a single virtue, but the distillation and culmination of all virtues, expressed at any given moment as a blend of fairness, kindness, gentleness, honesty, respect, courage, and love. The power to express any or all of these virtues at the appropriate moment indicates that a person has internally unified him- or herself into a state of compassion.

The heart is like a cauldron that we can use for combining all the virtues into the energy of compassion, the ultimate virtue and a necessary attribute for our evolving spiritual being (fig. 5.3). The basis of compassion is empathy (not sympathy, which is a weakness people show when the emotions of others easily affect them). Compassion elevates the consciousness beyond human weakness. When we have compassion, we can love unconditionally and thereby accept the world on its own terms without suffering.

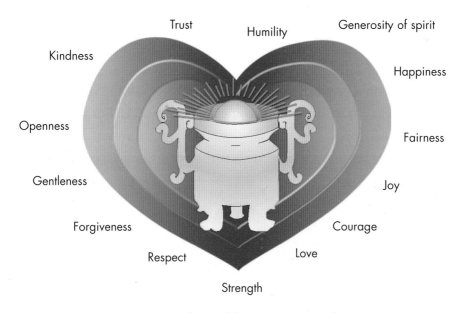

Fig. 5.3. Cauldron of the compassionate heart

THE VIRTUE OF LOVE

When studying the virtues, we must examine love as a category in itself to better understand its energetic influences. The Taoists view love as an internal energy of the heart rather than as a product of the mind. Although we generally think of love as a positive force, what we commonly call love can actually evoke more negativity in our lives than all the other negative energies combined. For example, we know that extreme love can quickly turn to hate of the most bitter and violent kind.

The misunderstanding of love can also create a vehicle that allows our negative emotions to drain our life force away in the form of self-sacrifice. While our personal supply of energy is limited, the loving energy of the universe is inexhaustible. When we know how to connect to this wellspring, we will always have enough love for ourselves and for others (fig. 5.4). Yet, if we don't learn how to tap into the higher force to enhance and replenish our supply, we often end up giving away more than we can afford. Eventually, this can cause us to drain out our sexual energy and burn out the love in our hearts. We expect love in a personal way from those who are close to us, and in a spiritual way from those who become our role models. But the words

Fig. 5.4. The compassionate heart

and actions of others almost never fulfill our needs. The question of what love is, has puzzled men and women for millennia. The answer can only be found within ourselves.

A major problem in our modern world is that we always look outside ourselves to fulfill our needs, without realizing that others are seeking fulfillment in the same way. Out of habit, we all seek love externally, without nurturing our own source of that energy within us. This leaves us with little to give. Logically, if others are also seeking love in the same way, they expect us to have enough loving energy to fulfill them. If we don't cultivate love within ourselves, however, we can drain their energies as they drain ours, until the relationship comes to an end. Success in any relationship depends on the ability of all the parties to share in an abundance of love that originates from both sources. Once we are full of love and life force, we can connect to the unlimited loving energy in the universe and share it abundantly with others.

Taoists say we cannot really love others until we can love ourselves. The stress of giving away freely what we don't have enough of can create blockages in the Microcosmic Orbit and can also block the unconditional love from Heaven and Earth. Because loving energy is accessible from within, we can resolve our primary need for love by using this energy first to replenish the internal organs and glands. Practices such as the Inner Smile help us achieve this.

While learning self-love, we should always remember that even the loving energy within us derives from the original force of the Wu Chi. This means that the heart's energy (where the loving energy resides) provides a connection to our divine source: Universal Love. The connection between inner and outer sources requires constant attention and alignment. We first have to cultivate love within ourselves to have the power to draw in unconditional love from Heaven, and gentleness and kindness from Mother Earth.

In Taoism, we believe that each organ has its own soul and spirit energy. By practicing love and respect to cultivate these aspects of the organs, the whole body improves and we learn to love the body as a whole. After learning self-love (which is not to be confused with egoism or narcissism) and connecting with the universal love, we become filled with loving energy to share with others. Practice is the key.

The Universal Tao system emphasizes this recycling, transforming, and refining of internal and external chi and of our emotional energy in particular. With the practice of the Inner Smile, we learn to detoxify the organs and let the virtue energy grow again (fig. 5.5). Transforming our internal energy in this way will also promote a higher vibratory rate and enhance our spiritual growth.

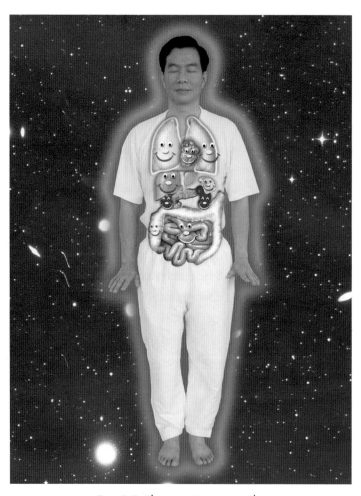

Fig. 5.5. The cosmic inner smile

Taoist Wisdom for Daily Life

Smile Away the Stress

Remember always to smile sincerely with your eyes and to fill your heart with love. This acts as a preventive medicine. When you are sad, angry, resentful, depressed, or anxious, your organs secrete poisons; but when you are happy and smiling, they produce a honeylike, health-giving secretion instead.

It is common knowledge that life today is very hectic. Ending the workday with a headache has become a way of life for many. With pressures building seemingly all around you and within you, "something has to be done." Oddly, the thing to do is not to do anything. When a trying situation arises, you have to learn not to be drawn in by it—no matter what it might be. The way to be able to do that is to smile. In that simple act the world is made over, and situations that would otherwise have been troublesome never seem to arise.

At first it may prove to be very difficult to comprehend the results of the Inner Smile, let alone to make it into a new experience, but with sufficient practice, you will find it to be an integral part of your life.

Wherever you are—standing, walking, or sitting—remember to relax and smile, to fill your heart with love, and to let the loving feeling spread throughout your whole body. It is so very simple and yet so very effective. Just cultivate a peaceful, loving heart; smile easily and your troubles will melt away.

Speak Thoughtfully

Speak less; choose carefully what to say and when and how to say it. Speaking appropriately can be a blessing to all, and speaking less conserves chi.

Worry Less—Take Action More

Spend less time thinking about the future and the past, because those are the things that worry builds on, and worry produces stress.

Try instead to concentrate on the present whenever you can— remember that the present moment happens and is not something that you make happen—and cultivate attitudes of forgiveness and activities of helpfulness in your daily life.

Cultivate Your Mental Power

Taoist methods involve the cultivation of generative and mental powers. The word for *mind* also means "heart" in many Asian languages, as it does in Chinese. When you develop to the stage of no longer being concerned with personal ambition, when you are able to forget yourself and cultivate your heart, you have at hand the means of being free from illness.

When you are ill and you meditate, do not think that you are meditating to escape from your illness. Instead, simply concentrate on a prescribed point or method, and everything else will drop away.

Control Your Sex Life— Do Not Let It Control You

Curb your sexual activity. Too frequent ejaculation will greatly reduce your store of chi and your ability to concentrate.

The mind is troubled by what is fed to it through the eyes, ears, mouth, nose, and mind—that is, the senses. When we are young and are exposed to sexually stimulating reading matter, for example, we are not equipped to deal properly with it in a way that would conserve our energy. Therefore, it is advised that you concentrate on your daily practice and avoid "distractions."

Respect Your Head—Warm Your Feet

Regard your head with the greatest respect. Think of it as a temple of God and of the mind. See it as the temple of the soul and the main control of all the vital organs. There is a rule of thumb to abide by, which is "Cool head, warm feet." Abiding by this rule will insure you against collecting too much power in your head, thereby possibly causing you discomfort and even illness. When power goes to the head, high blood pressure can develop. Directing the power down to the feet can relieve the pressure, and keeping the feet warm can guard you against heart attack. So rub your feet and keep them warm. When you finish, you must always store the energy in the navel and keep it warm.

Keep Your Neck Warm

The neck has many important blood vessels and nerves and connects to that very important part of you, the head. So treat it well, too; keep it warm and loose by pervading it with a smile.

Wisdom in Eating

Do not overeat. If you eat until you are too full and then lie down or sit for a long time, this practice will surely shorten your life.

Stop eating before satiation, and then take a leisurely stroll; and do not eat at all at night before retiring.

If you have eaten too much, be careful not to drink too much water and not to gulp it down suddenly.

Indigestion follows when you eat to satiation after having been hungry for a long time.

Eat small amounts of food and eat more frequently. In this way you will be assured of proper digestion and of not overtaxing your five organs.

When eating, eat hot foods first, then warm, and if there are no cold foods, drink some cold water. Always, before eating, inhale slightly and swallow some air.

In general, cooked food is better than uncooked, and eating a little is better than eating a lot.

Too many raw vegetables can upset a person's healthy color.

Do not eat raw fruit on an empty stomach, because it heats above the diaphragm.

Avoid Excess in These Things

Walking too long harms the tendons; sitting too long harms the flesh; standing too long harms the bones; lying down too long harms vital energy; and gazing too long harms the blood.

Too much anger, grief, pity, or melancholy is harmful, as is too much joy or pleasure. Prolonged suffering is harmful; prolonged abstinence from sexual activity is harmful; prolonged anxiety is harmful. In short, to neglect moderation is harmful.

Try not to use your senses too much. Don't look at or listen to anything for too long at a time. Whenever the senses are used excessively, sickness can result.

You can exhaust your vital energy by too frequent sexual activity.

If you overindulge with too much food and drink, you will cause yourself ill health.

Seasonal Health Care

During winter, see to it that your feet are warm and allow your head to be cool. In the spring and autumn permit both your head and feet to be cool.

When lying down in spring and summer have your head face east, whereas in autumn and winter it should face west.

In the summer and autumn, go to sleep early and arise early; in the winter, retire early and arise late; in the spring, go to sleep while there is daylight and arise early.

Eat more pungent foods in the spring, more sour foods in the summer, more bitter foods in the autumn, and less salty foods in the winter, but do not be excessive in doing this.

Other Tips from the Tao for Good Health

To prolong your life and avoid illness, practice swallowing your saliva many times a day. To swallow saliva is to increase its essence. When it is not swallowed it loses strength.

At dawn, midday, during the afternoon, at twilight, and at midnight, clean your teeth and rinse your mouth seven times. This will lengthen your life and strengthen your bones, teeth, muscles, nails, and hair.

Do not expose yourself to the wind after bathing or perspiring.

When you are ill, do not lie with your head to the north.

When ill and perspiring, do not drink cold water, as this will damage your heart and stomach.

To be free of sickness, a master squats to urinate before eating and stands to urinate after eating.

When sleeping, bend the knees and lie on your side. This increases your vital energy.

Right after awakening from sleep, excessive talking robs you of vital energy.

Replace the unpurified chi of your body with pure original chi, by practicing the Microcosmic Orbit and by opening all of the thirty-two routes.

Joy increases the chi. With great joy, the vital chi soars. Great sadness causes the flow of chi to stop.

Please the divinities within, and you may in time progress toward immortality.

 Acknowledgments

We extend our gratitude to the many generations of Taoist masters who have passed on their special lineage as an unbroken oral transmission over thousands of years. We particularly thank Taoist Master I Yun (Yi Eng) for his openness in transmitting the formulas of Taoist Inner Alchemy.

We offer our eternal gratitude to our parents and teachers for their many gifts to us. Remembering them brings joy and satisfaction to our continued efforts in presenting the Universal Tao system.

We also wish to thank the thousands of unknown men and women of the Chinese healing arts who developed many of the methods and ideas presented in this book.

We thank the many contributors essential to this book's final form: The editorial and production staff at Inner Traditions/Destiny Books for their efforts to clarify the text and produce a handsome new edition of the book, Victoria Sant'Ambrogio for her line edit of the new edition, and the artist, Juan Li, for his fine illustrations.

We wish to thank the following people who contributed to the earlier editions of this book: Dena Saxer, Udon, Lee Holden, Wilbert Wils, Jean Chilton, Jettaya Phaobtong, and Saumya Comer. We also thank our Thai Production team, Raruen Keawpadung, Saysunee Yongyod, Udon Jandee, and Saniem Chaisarn.

About the Author

Mantak Chia has been studying the Taoist approach to life since childhood. His mastery of this ancient knowledge, enhanced by his study of other disciplines, has resulted in the development of the Universal Tao system, which is now being taught throughout the world.

Mantak Chia was born in Thailand to Chinese parents in 1944. When he was six years old, he learned from Buddhist monks how to sit and "still the mind." While in grammar school, he learned traditional Thai boxing, and soon went on to acquire considerable skill in aikido, yoga, and tai chi. His studies of the Taoist way of life began in earnest when he was a student in Hong Kong, ultimately leading to his mastery of a wide variety of esoteric disciplines, with the guidance of several masters, including Master I Yun, Master Meugi, Master Cheng Yao Lun, and Master Pan Yu. To better understand the mechanisms behind healing energy, he also studied Western anatomy and medical sciences.

Master Chia has taught his system of healing and energizing practices to tens of thousands of students and trained more than two thousand instructors and practitioners throughout the world. He has established centers for Taoist study and training in many countries around the globe. In June of 1990, he was honored by the International Congress of Chinese Medicine and Qi Gong (Chi Kung), which named him the Qi Gong Master of the Year.

The Universal Tao System and Training Center

THE UNIVERSAL TAO SYSTEM

The ultimate goal of Taoist practice is to transcend physical boundaries through the development of the soul and the spirit within the human. That is also the guiding principle behind the Universal Tao, a practical system of self-development that enables individuals to complete the harmonious evolution of their physical, mental, and spiritual bodies. Through a series of ancient Chinese meditative and internal energy exercises, the practitioner learns to increase physical energy, release tension, improve health, practice self-defense, and gain the ability to heal him- or herself and others. In the process of creating a solid foundation of health and well-being in the physical body, the practitioner also creates the basis for developing his or her spiritual potential by learning to tap into the natural energies of the sun, moon, earth, stars, and other environmental forces.

The Universal Tao practices are derived from ancient techniques rooted in the processes of nature. They have been gathered and integrated into a coherent, accessible system for well-being that works directly with the life force, or chi, that flows through the meridian system of the body.

Master Chia has spent years developing and perfecting techniques for teaching these traditional practices to students around the world through ongoing classes, workshops, private instruction, and healing sessions, as well as through books and video and audio products. Further information can be obtained at www.universal-tao.com.

THE UNIVERSAL TAO TRAINING CENTER

The Tao Garden Resort and Training Center in northern Thailand is the home of Master Chia and serves as the worldwide headquarters for Universal Tao activities. This integrated wellness, holistic health, and training center is situated on eighty acres surrounded by the beautiful Himalayan foothills near the historic walled city of Chiang Mai. The serene setting includes flower and herb gardens ideal for meditation, open-air pavilions for practicing Chi Kung, and a health and fitness spa.

The center offers classes all year long, as well as summer and winter retreats. It can accommodate two hundred students, and group leasing can be arranged. For information worldwide on courses, books, products, and other resources, see below.

RESOURCES

Universal Healing Tao Center
274 Moo 7, Laung Nua, Doi Saket, Chiang Mai, 50220, Thailand
Tel: (66)(53) 921-200
E-mail: universaltao@universal-tao.com
Web site: www.universal-tao.com

For information on retreats and the health spa, contact:
Tao Garden Health Spa & Resort
E-mail: reservations@tao-garden.com
Web site: www.tao-garden.com

Good Chi • Good Heart • Good Intention

Index

Page numbers in *italics* refer to illustrations.

BOOKS OF RELATED INTEREST

Chi Self-Massage
The Taoist Way of Rejuvenation
by Mantak Chia

Healing Light of the Tao
Foundational Practices to Awaken Chi Energy
by Mantak Chia

Healing Love through the Tao
Cultivating Female Sexual Energy
by Mantak Chia

Craniosacral Chi Kung
Integrating Body and Emotion in the Cosmic Flow
by Mantak Chia and Joyce Thom

Pi Gu Chi Kung
Inner Alchemy Energy Fasting
by Mantak Chia and Christine Harkness-Giles

Chi Nei Tsang
Chi Massage for the Vital Organs
by Mantak Chia

Life Pulse Massage
Taoist Techniques for Enhanced Circulation and Detoxification
by Mantak Chia and Aisha Sieburth

The Six Healing Sounds
Taoist Techniques for Balancing Chi
by Mantak Chia

Inner Traditions • Bear & Company
P.O. Box 388
Rochester, VT 05767
1-800-246-8648
www.InnerTraditions.com

Or contact your local bookseller